Matzah MEALS

A Passover Cookbook for Kids

Judy Tabs
& Barbara Steinberg

pictures by
Bill Hauser

KAR-BEN
PUBLISHING

CONTENTS

MEALS FROM AROUND THE WORLD 45

DESSERTS AND SNACKS 51

SHAKES AND COOLERS 61

METRIC CONVERSIONS

MASS (weight)

1 ounce (oz.)	= 28 grams (g)
8 ounces	= 227 g
1 pound (lb.) or 16 oz.	= 0.45 kilograms (kg)
2.2 lbs.	= 1 kg

LIQUID VOLUME

1 teaspoon (tsp.)	= 5 milliliters (ml)
1 tablespoon (tbsp.)	= 15 ml
1 fluid ounce (oz.)	= 30 ml
1 cup (c.)	= 240 ml
1 pint (pt.)	= 480 ml
1 quart (qt.)	= 0.95 liters (l)
1 gallon (gal.)	= 3.80 l

WELCOME!

... to the second and expanded edition of the Passover cookbook just for kids. We've included old favorites and added more than a dozen new recipes to try and enjoy. After you've sampled Matzah Tostada, Lox and Onion Matzah Brei, and melt-in-your-mouth Chocolate Chip Cookies, you'll agree that Passover eating is fun!

BEFORE YOU BEGIN...

We know you're eager to get started, but please take a minute to read these tips. They'll save you time in the end, and insure that your Passover foods turn out just right.

- Ask permission to use the kitchen. If you are using sharp knives, the blender, food processor, or stove, make sure that an older person is close by to supervise your cooking.

- Wash your hands, and wear an apron or washable work clothes.

- Read the recipe carefully and check to see that you have all the ingredients.

- Assemble all ingredients and equipment. Recheck the recipe to make sure you have everything.

- Clear a space to work. Keep a sponge handy for unexpected spills.

- Remember these safety tips: Use potholders to handle hot dishes. Turn pot handles toward the back of the stove, so you don't accidentally knock over a hot pot. Pick up knives by the handle, not the blade, and always cut away from yourself. Always wash fresh fruits and vegetables.

- When you're finished, turn off the stove or oven; put away all food; and wash, dry, and put away all equipment. Wipe the counters and sweep the floor. Remember, good cooks always leave the kitchen neat and clean.

USING THIS COOKBOOK

E-Z SYMBOLS

means very easy. No cooking or baking is required. Even your little brother can help.

means you may have to chop, slice, use a blender or food processor, or bake.

means you must use a hot stove to boil or fry. An adult should be present when you make these recipes.

MEAT/DAIRY/PARVE SYMBOLS

M is a meat recipe

D is a dairy recipe

P is a parve recipe (may be eaten with either meat or dairy)

Sometimes a dairy dish can be made parve just by using parve margarine instead of butter. These recipes have the symbols D/P. All packaged foods included in the recipes are available labeled "Kosher for Passover." If your family keeps a kosher home, it is important to use the correct dishes and pots in preparing your recipe.

EQUIPMENT

Cooking goes faster when you have everything ready. Check the equipment list under the ingredients before you start each recipe. These pictures will help you find what you need.

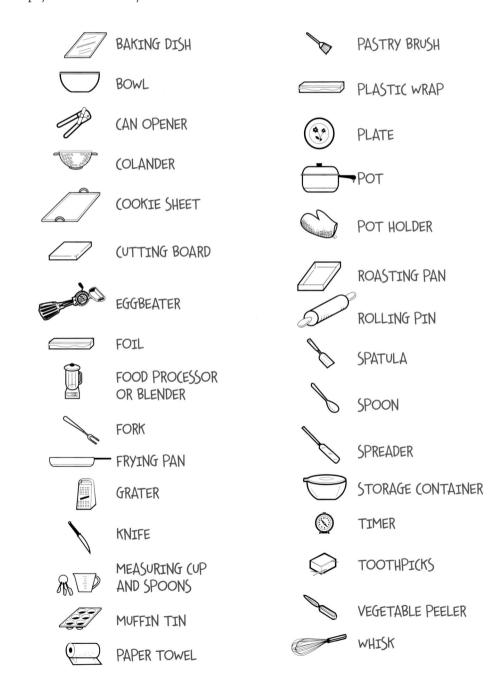

BAKING DISH

BOWL

CAN OPENER

COLANDER

COOKIE SHEET

CUTTING BOARD

EGGBEATER

FOIL

FOOD PROCESSOR OR BLENDER

FORK

FRYING PAN

GRATER

KNIFE

MEASURING CUP AND SPOONS

MUFFIN TIN

PAPER TOWEL

PASTRY BRUSH

PLASTIC WRAP

PLATE

POT

POT HOLDER

ROASTING PAN

ROLLING PIN

SPATULA

SPOON

SPREADER

STORAGE CONTAINER

TIMER

TOOTHPICKS

VEGETABLE PEELER

WHISK

THE KIDS' COMPLETE SEDER MENU

Gefilte Fish Kabobs (p. 18)

Horseradish Salsa (p. 47)

Chicken Soup with Matzah Balls (pp. 16–17)

Carrot-Raisin Salad (p. 34)

Oven-Baked Chicken (p. 42)

Peach Kugel (p. 37)

Strawberry Layer Cake (p. 56)

Grape Spritzer (p. 63)

THE STORY OF PASSOVER

Passover lasts for a whole week. The holiday begins with a special meal called a seder. We read the story of how the Jewish people were freed from slavery in Egypt. We use a book called a Haggadah.

The Haggadah tells us that many years ago in the land of Egypt, there lived a mean king called Pharaoh. The Jewish people who lived in Egypt were slaves. They had to work very hard building cities and palaces for Pharaoh. Pharaoh was especially mean to Jewish children. One mother put her baby boy in a basket in the river so Pharaoh wouldn't find him. When Pharaoh's daughter saw the baby, she took him out of the river and saved him. She named him Moses.

When Moses grew up, he saw how cruelly the Jewish slaves were treated and decided to leave Egypt. He became a shepherd in a faraway land. One day, while he was watching his sheep, he heard the voice of God telling him to go back to Egypt and free the Jewish people. Moses went to Pharaoh and asked him to let the Jewish people go. Pharaoh refused. God was angry and punished Pharaoh ten times. Finally, Pharaoh told Moses to take his people out of Egypt.

The Jews left in a hurry and didn't have time to bake their bread in an oven. They put the dough on their backs, and while they were walking, the sun baked it into hard crackers (matzah). Moses led the Jewish people out of Egypt, across the sea, and into the desert. The Jews were happy to be saved. Moses told them to celebrate Passover every year to remember that once they were slaves, but God helped them become free.

SEDER SYMBOLS

Special foods on the seder table remind us of the Passover story:

MATZAH
Reminds us that the Jews had to leave Egypt quickly and had no time to bake bread.

GREENS
Parsley or celery—remind us that Passover comes in the spring when everything begins to grow.

SALT WATER
Reminds us of the tears of the Jewish slaves in Egypt.

CHAROSET
A mixture of apples, nuts, and wine—reminds us of the mortar the Jews used to make bricks to build Pharaoh's cities.

MAROR
A bitter vegetable like horseradish—reminds us of the bitter way Pharaoh treated the Jewish people.

ROASTED EGG
Reminds us of the new life that grows in spring.

BONE
Reminds us of the roasted lamb the Jewish people ate when they celebrated the first Passover.

WINE
A symbol of holiday joy.

ELIJAH'S CUP
There is a legend that the prophet Elijah visits each seder to wish us a year of peace.

MIRIAM'S CUP
We fill a cup to symbolize a well to honor Moses' sister Miriam. When the Jewish people were in the desert, Miriam was a source of strength and comfort to them.

SETTING THE SEDER TABLE

The seder is a wonderful celebration, and it's fun to make our dinner table beautiful. Help choose a pretty tablecloth or placemats. Buy fresh flowers, or make colorful paper ones for a centerpiece. This is what you'll need for the seder:

AT EACH PLACE:

- Plate, silverware, napkin
- Wine glass
- Haggadah

ON THE TABLE:

- Candles to welcome the holiday
- Wine or grape juice—enough for four cups for each person
- Three matzah—covered with a matzah cover or napkin
- Cups of salt water for dipping the parsley
- Elijah and/or Miriam's cup

FOR THE LEADER OF THE SEDER:

- A pillow for reclining

FOR THE SEDER PLATE:

- Greens
- Charoset
- Bitter herb
- Roasted Egg
- Roasted Bone

(Recipes for these foods are on pages 11–12)

ROASTED EGG AND BONE

WHAT YOU NEED:

egg

shankbone (or other bone)

Pin
Roasting pan
Pot holder
Timer

WHAT YOU DO:

1. Prick the egg with a pin to let steam escape while cooking.

2. Put egg and bone on baking sheet and roast at 300° for 1 hour.

HORSERADISH

WHAT YOU NEED:

½ lb. horseradish root

1–2 beets, fresh or canned (optional)

2 Tbsp. vinegar

2 Tbsp. sugar

¼ c. water

1 tsp. salt

Vegetable peeler
Knife and cutting board
Blender or food processor
Measuring spoon and cup

WHAT YOU DO:

1. Peel horseradish root and cut into chunks. If you want red horseradish, peel beets and cut into chunks, also.

2. Put chunks into blender or food processor. Add vinegar and sugar.

3. Blend a few seconds until chopped. Don't overblend.

Note: Strong horseradish may irritate your eyes.

CHAROSET

WHAT YOU NEED:

8 apples

1 tsp. cinnamon

½ cup chopped nuts

2 Tbsp. sweet red wine

Bowl
Vegetable peeler
Measuring spoon
Knife and chopper

WHAT YOU DO:

1. Peel apples, remove cores, and slice into a bowl.

2. Add nuts and cinnamon, and chop until fine.

3. Add wine and mix.

Serves 6–8

GREENS (KARPAS)

WHAT YOU NEED:

Parsley, celery, or lettuce

Knife and cutting board

WHAT YOU DO:

Cut into bite-size pieces and place on the seder plate.

SALT WATER

WHAT YOU NEED:

1 cup cold water

1 tsp. salt

Measuring cup and spoon

WHAT YOU DO:

Put cold water in small pitcher or cup. Add salt. You may wish to make several cups to place around the table.

MATZAH*

WHAT YOU NEED:

2 cups unbleached flour

½ cup water (more if needed)

Mixing bowl and spoon
Rolling pin
Baking sheet
Fork
Spatula
Pot holder
Timer

WHAT YOU DO:

1. Preheat oven to 450°.

2. Place flour in bowl.

3. Make a well (hole) in the middle of the flour and pour in water. Mix.

4. Add more water as needed until all the flour is mixed. Use your hands . . . it's fun! Knead dough until soft, not sticky.

5. Roll into a ball. Divide into quarters.

6. Roll or pat each quarter into a circle. Place matzah on baking sheet and prick all over with a fork. Bake for 5 minutes on each side, or until edges are golden.

Makes

*The requirements for making matzah are very strict, and some rabbis do not consider home-baked matzah "kosher" for Passover.

SEDER TABLE CRAFTS

SEDER PLATES

Decorate paper plates with Passover symbols. Glue foil muffin cups to each one, and fill with individual portions of parsley, charoset, egg, maror, and a small bone. Give a seder plate to every guest.

KIDDUSH CUP OR CUP FOR ELIJAH OR MIRIAM

Cover two paper cups (one size apart) with foil. Glue them bottom to bottom. The smaller one is the stem of your wine cup.

PASSOVER PLACEMATS

Cut labels from matzah, wine, gefilte fish, and other Passover foods. Arrange them in a collage on pieces of construction paper. Cover on both sides with clear adhesive paper. The placemats may be wiped clean and stored for future holiday meals.

PLACE CARDS

Fold index cards in half. Decorate with pictures of Passover symbols or spring flowers, and write each guest's name on a card.

MATZAH COVER

Sew four pieces of felt or cloth together leaving one side open to insert the three matzot. To decorate the top cloth, color with crayon, cover with waxed paper, and iron to set the design. Make a matching afikomen bag.

PILLOW COVER

Draw, paint, or embroider Passover symbols on a special pillow case to cover the pillow used for reclining at the seder.

TEN PLAGUES

Add some drama to your seder. Bring the 10 plagues to life:

Blood: Use red food coloring in a glass of water.

Frogs: Try plastic ones or stickers.

Lice: White rice. If you want, add eyes with a black magic marker.

Beasts: Animal masks or toy dinosaurs

Boils: Color round band-aids with red marker.

Cattle disease: Plastic cows colored green

Hail: Styrofoam packing pellets work great.

Locusts: Plastic grasshoppers

Darkness: Blindfolds

Death of firstborn: This one is tricky, but you can use skeletons, black armbands, or toe-tags.

MATZAH MAGNETS

Post your shopping list or favorite recipes on the refrigerator with matzah magnets. Glue buttons, fabric scraps, or bits of yarn onto broken pieces of matzah. Spray with varnish or shellac, and glue magnets to the backs.

SOUPS AND APPETIZERS

CHICKEN SOUP FOR BEGINNERS

WHAT YOU NEED:

2 chicken boullion cubes

1 quart (4 cups) water

2 peeled carrots

2 celery stalks

½ tsp. dry dill

Pot with cover
Measuring cup and spoon
Vegetable peeler
Knife and cutting board
Pot holder
Timer

WHAT YOU DO:

1. Put the boullion cubes in the water and bring to a boil.

2. Wash and cut up carrots and celery. Add to boiling soup.

3. Add dill.

4. Cover and cook over low heat (simmer) until vegetables are soft, about 20 minutes.

Serves

CHICKEN SOUP FOR EXPERTS

WHAT YOU NEED:

cut up chicken

quarts (8 cups) water

celery stalks, including leaves

onion

—4 peeled carrots

Tbsp. salt

—3 shakes of pepper

bay leaf (optional)

arge pot with cover

Measuring cup and spoons

egetable peeler

nife and cutting board

trainer and storage container

ot holder

imer

WHAT YOU DO:

1. Cover chicken with water and bring to a boil.

2. Add vegetables and spices.

3. Cover and cook over low heat (simmer) for 1½ hours, until chicken is soft.

4. Cool and strain. Remove skin and bones from chicken and discard. Return vegetables and chicken to soup.

5. Soup is best if refrigerated overnight. Skim off fat before reheating and serving.

Serves 8

E-Z MATZAH BALLS

WHAT YOU NEED:

Tbsp. oil

eggs, slightly beaten

½ cup matzah meal

tsp. salt

Tbsp. water

owl

Measuring cup and spoons

ork, spoon

lastic wrap

arge pot with cover

ot holder

imer

WHAT YOU DO:

1. Mix oil and eggs together in a bowl.

2. Add matzah meal and salt. Mix well. Add water and mix again.

3. Cover with plastic wrap and refrigerate for ½ hour.

4. Fill large pot with 6 cups of water and bring to a boil.

5. Wet your hands and take about a tablespoon of the mixture and roll into a ball. Drop into boiling water. Reduce heat to a slow boil. Cook covered for 30–40 minutes.

6. Remove from water and serve in chicken soup.

GEFILTE FISH KABOBS [P]

WHAT YOU NEED:

1 jar gefilte fish tidbits
1 small can pineapple chunks
Cherry tomatoes
Lettuce
Horseradish (optional)

Toothpicks
Can opener
Fork or spoon
Serving platter

WHAT YOU DO:

1. Place a fish tidbit, a pineapple chunk, and a cherry tomato on a toothpick.

2. Arrange kabobs on a bed of lettuce Serve with horseradish.

VEGGIES AND DIP [D/P] [D/P]

DIPPERS:

Cherry tomatoes
Broccoli and cauliflower cut into
   florettes
Carrots and celery cut into sticks
Cucumber slices

Bowl
Fork, spoon, knife, and cutting board
Measuring cup and spoon
Vegetable peeler
Can opener

PINEAPPLE DIP
Mix ¼ cup crushed pineapple with 2 teaspoons of mayonnaise.

ONION DIP
Mix 1 cup sour cream with a package of Passover onion soup mix.

CUCUMBER DIP
Mash 8 oz. package cream cheese* with dash of grated onion and one grated and strained cucumber.

CHEESY-NUT DIP
Mash 3 oz. package cream cheese* with ¼ cup chopped walnuts.

*Let cream cheese soften at room temperature for about an hour before using.

BREAKFAST, BRUNCH AND LUNCH

JAM-FILLED MUFFINS 🥘🥘

WHAT YOU NEED:

MUFFINS:

6 large eggs

¾ cup oil

1 cup light brown sugar

½ cup matzah meal

1 cup cake meal

2 tsp. vanilla

1 tsp. cinnamon

pinch of salt

1 Tbsp. orange juice

6 tsp. strawberry jam (not jelly)

STREUSEL TOPPING:

½ cup brown sugar

3 Tbsp. potato starch

1½ tsp. cinnamon

¾ cup chopped nuts

2 Tbsp. oil

Measuring cups and spoons
Large and small bowls
Mixing spoon or whisk
Muffin tin
Non-stick spray or muffin tin liners
Pot holder
Timer

WHAT YOU DO:

1. Preheat oven to 350°.

2. Spray muffin tin with non-stick spray or place liners in the cups.

3. Whisk eggs in large bowl. Add all ingredients except jam. Mix until blended. Do not overmix.

4. Fill muffin cups ¾ full. Spoon ½ tsp. jam into center of each muffin. Lightly press into batter.

5. Mix together ingredients for streusel topping until crumbly. Sprinkle some on top of each muffin.

6. Bake for 25 minutes or until toothpick comes out clean.

Makes 12 muffins

GRANOLA

WHAT YOU NEED:

4 cups matzah farfel

½ cup nuts

¼ cup shredded coconut

½ cup honey

½ cup oil

½ cup raisins

Measuring cup

Mixing bowl and spoon

Baking sheet

Timer

Pot holder

Storage container with cover

WHAT YOU DO:

1. Preheat oven to 350°.

2. Mix farfel, nuts, and coconut in a bowl. Add honey and oil, and mix well.

3. Spread mixture on baking sheet. Bake 30 minutes. Stir frequently. Cool.

4. Add raisins and mix. Store in covered container.

8–10 servings

SCRAMBLED EGGS

WHAT YOU NEED:

2 eggs

2 Tbsp. cold water or milk

1 Tbsp. butter or margarine

Salt and pepper to taste

Small bowl and fork

Frying pan

Spatula

Measuring spoon

Pot holder

WHAT YOU DO:

1. Beat eggs and water (or milk) until fluffy. Add salt and pepper.

2. Put butter or margarine in frying pan and melt over medium heat.

3. Pour eggs into pan and stir until set.

Serves 1

MATZAH MEAL LATKES

WHAT YOU NEED:

½ cup matzah meal

½ tsp. salt

1 tsp. sugar

3 eggs

¾ cup cold water

Oil for frying

Measuring cups and spoons
Mixing bowl
Frying pan (or griddle) and spatula
Eggbeater/mixer (for extra light latkes)
Pot holder

WHAT YOU DO:

1. Mix matzah meal, salt, and sugar together in a bowl.

2. Add eggs and water, and mix well.

3. Heat oil in frying pan. Drop by tablespoons into pan, and brown on both sides.

*FOR EXTRA-LIGHT LATKES:

1. After step 1 above, separate the eggs (let an adult help you). Beat yolks and add water. Add matzah meal mixture to yolks. Let stand for one hour.

2. Beat egg whites until stiff, and add to batter. Fry as directed above.

Serves 3—

COTTAGE CHEESE PANCAKES

WHAT YOU NEED:

1 cup cottage cheese

2 eggs, beaten

¼ cup matzah meal

1 Tbsp. sugar

¼ tsp. salt

Butter or margarine for frying

Bowl and spoon
Measuring cup and spoons
Frying pan and spatula
Pot holder

WHAT YOU DO:

1. Mix all ingredients except butter in a bowl.

2. Melt butter or margarine in frying pan over medium heat.

3. Drop batter by tablespoons onto hot frying pan. Brown on both sides.

4. Serve with jelly or sour cream.

Serves 2—

BANANA PANCAKES

WHAT YOU NEED:

eggs

⅓ cup matzah meal

Tbsp. cake meal

¼ cup sour cream

¼ cup cottage cheese

ripe banana, mashed

Salt to taste

Oil or butter for frying

Mixing bowl and spoon
Measuring cups and spoons
Frying pan and spatula
Pot holder

WHAT YOU DO:

1. Mix all ingredients except oil in a bowl.

2. Heat oil in frying pan over medium heat.

3. Drop batter by tablespoons into pan and brown on both sides.

4. Serve with jelly or sour cream.

Serves 3–4

FRENCH TOAST

WHAT YOU NEED:

I egg
I Tbsp. milk
Pinch of salt
I matzah
I Tbsp. butter or margarine

Mixing bowl and spoon
Measuring spoon
Frying pan and spatula
Pot holder

WHAT YOU DO:

1. Beat egg with milk and salt.

2. Break matzah into quarters and dip each piece into the mixture.

3. Melt butter or margarine in frying pan. Fry matzah on both sides until brown. Serve hot with sugar, syrup, honey, or butter.

Serves 1—

MAPLE SYRUP

MATZAH BREI

WHAT YOU NEED:

4 matzah
3 eggs, beaten
1/2 cup milk
3 Tbsp. oil or margarine

Measuring cup and spoons
Mixing bowl and spoon
Frying pan and spatula
Pot holder

WHAT YOU DO:

1. Crumble matzah into bowl. Add eggs and milk, and mix well. Let stand for five minutes to soften matzah.

2. Heat oil in a frying pan. Put matzah mixture into pan and fry on both sides until crisp. Top with jelly or a mixture of cinnamon and sugar.

Serves 3—4

LOX & ONION MATZAH BREI

WHAT YOU NEED:

4 matzah broken into 2" pieces
3 eggs
1 small onion, minced
4 Tbsp. cream cheese, softened
Salt and pepper to taste
1/4 cup lox, diced
Margarine or butter for frying

Measuring cup and spoon
Colander
Mixing bowl and spoon
Knife and cutting board
Frying pan and spatula
Pot holder

WHAT YOU DO:

1. Place matzah in a colander and pour hot water over it. Squeeze out liquid.

2. Beat eggs in a bowl, and add matzah, onion, cream cheese, salt, and pepper.

3. Heat margarine in pan. Pour batter into pan. Cook over moderate heat until bottom is set. Add lox, scramble, and cook until done.

Serves 2—3

PASSOVER SANDWICH ROLLS

WHAT YOU NEED:

½ cup water

⅓ cup oil

1 cup matzah meal

2 tsp. sugar

¼ tsp. salt

2 eggs

Nonstick spray or oil for cookie sheet

Measuring cup and spoons
Mixing bowl and spoon
Pot
Baking sheet
Pot holder
Timer

WHAT YOU DO:

1. Preheat oven to 375°.

2. Put water and oil in a pot, and bring to a boil. Cool.

3. Add matzah meal, sugar, and salt, and mix well.

4. Add eggs, one at a time, and mix well. Let stand for 15 minutes.

5. Grease hands with oil and form mixture into 6–8 balls. Place on oiled cookie sheet and flatten.

6. Bake for 40 minutes or until golden brown.

Makes 6–8 roll

SANDWICH SPREADS

CREAM CHEESE AND JELLY:
Spread cream cheese on matzah or roll. Top with your favorite jam or jelly.

HONEY BUTTER:
Mix ¼ cup of softened butter or margarine with 4 tablespoons of honey. Spread on matzah, rolls, or Passover pancakes.

CINNAMON/SUGAR:
Spread matzah or roll with butter or margarine. Mix ¼ cup sugar with ¼ teaspoon cinnamon and sprinkle some on top.

ONION:
Cut an onion in half and rub the cut edge over matzah. Sprinkle with salt and pepper, and toast in warm oven. Spread with butter or margarine and serve warm.

SANDWICH FILLINGS

TUNA SALAD

WHAT YOU NEED:
1 can tuna fish
2 Tbsp. mayonnaise
1 stalk celery, diced (optional)
1 small onion, diced (optional)

Can opener   Knife and cutting board
Bowl and spoon   Measuring spoon

WHAT YOU DO:
Put tuna in a bowl. Mix with mayonnaise (and onion/celery).

Serves 2–3

EGG SALAD

WHAT YOU NEED:
2 eggs
2 Tbsp. mayonnaise
Salt and pepper

Pot
Knife and fork
Measuring spoon
Bowl

WHAT YOU DO:
1. Put eggs in pot and cover with cold water. Bring to a boil. Turn off heat and let eggs sit 20 minutes. Run under cold water to cool.

2. Peel eggs. Cut into quarters, and put in a bowl. Mash with mayonnaise, salt, and pepper.

Serves 2

GRILLED CHEESE SANDWICH

WHAT YOU NEED:

Matzah

Butter or margarine

Sliced cheese

Baking sheet
Knife
Pot holder

WHAT YOU DO:

1. Preheat oven to 400°.

2. Butter matzah and top with sliced cheese. Put on baking sheet and place in hot oven for a minute or two until cheese melts.

Serves

"UNSANDWICHES"

WHAT YOU NEED:

Bowl
Knife and cutting board
Measuring cup and spoon

APPLE

Cut an apple into wedges. Remove core. Spread wedges with cream cheese. Top with jelly.

WALNUT

Add ¼ teaspoon brown sugar and ½ cup raisins to 3 oz. softened cream cheese. Spread some on half of a walnut. Cover with the other half.

BANANA

Peel a banana and slice in half the long way. Spread jam on one half. Top with other half. Cut into bite-size pieces.

FRUITS AND VEGGIES

BABY MOSES SALAD ▢▢

WHAT YOU NEED:

Basket — Lettuce leaf
Body — Fresh or canned peach half
Arms and legs — Small celery sticks
Head — Large marshmallow
Mouth — Slice of red pepper
Hair — Shredded cheese
Eyes and nose — Raisins

Plate
Knife and cutting board

WHAT YOU DO:

Place peach half and marshmallow on large lettuce leaf. Decorate with other ingredients.

Serves

WALDORF SALAD ▢▢

WHAT YOU NEED:

1 can tuna, drained
1$\frac{1}{4}$ cup diced apple
2 Tbsp. lemon juice
$\frac{1}{4}$ cup finely chopped celery
2 Tbsp. chopped nuts
3 Tbsp. of mayonnaise or salad dressing

Can opener
Measuring cup and spoons
Mixing bowl and spoon
Knife and cutting board

WHAT YOU DO:

1. Mix tuna and apple in a bowl.

2. Sprinkle with lemon juice.

3. Add remaining ingredients and mix well.

Serves 2—

FRUIT KABOBS

WHAT YOU NEED:

Any or all of the following fruits:

Apple chunks

Orange sections

Grapes

Pineapple cubes

Melon balls

Dried prunes or apricots

Knife and cutting board
Toothpicks
Serving plate

WHAT YOU DO:

Select two or three pieces of fruit and place them on a toothpick. Arrange kabobs on serving plate.

APPLESAUCE

P P

WHAT YOU NEED:

8 tart apples

1–2 tsp. cinnamon

1 cup water

½ cup sugar

Vegetable peeler

Knife and cutting board

Measuring cup and spoon

Pot and mixing spoon

Pot holder

Fork

WHAT YOU DO:

1. Wash, peel, and slice apples. Put in a pot with water and bring to a boil.

2. Cover and simmer about 20 minutes or until apples are soft.

3. Add sugar and cinnamon, and mash with a fork.

4. Serve warm or cold.

Serves 6—

CRANBERRY RELISH P

WHAT YOU NEED:

2 cans whole cranberry sauce

2 cans crushed pineapple

1 package frozen strawberries, thawed

1 can mandarin oranges

Colander

Can opener

Bowl and spoon

Plastic wrap

WHAT YOU DO:

1. Pour all ingredients into colander and drain.*

2. Transfer fruit to a bowl and mix together. Cover with plastic wrap, and refrigerate before serving.

Serves 10–12

*You may wish to reserve juices for another use.

FRUIT COMPOTE P P

WHAT YOU NEED:

3 cups of sliced fresh or canned fruit (pineapple, peaches, pears, apples, oranges, grapes, apricots, etc.)

1 Tbsp. lemon juice

3 Tbsp. honey

Glass bowl

Colander

Spoon

Knife and cutting board

Measuring cup and spoon

Plastic wrap

WHAT YOU DO:

1. Drain canned fruit in colander. Put in bowl.

2. Slice fresh fruit and add it to bowl.

3. Stir in lemon juice and honey.

4. Cover with plastic wrap and refrigerate before serving.

Serves 4–6

CARROT-RAISIN SALAD

WHAT YOU NEED:

1 bag (1 lb.) carrots

1 cup raisins

½ cup mayonnaise

Vegetable peeler
Measuring cup
Food processor, blender, or grater
Mixing bowl and spoon
Knife and cutting board

WHAT YOU DO:

1. Wash and peel carrots. Cut into slices.

2. Shred carrot slices using food processor, blender, or grater.

3. Combine shredded carrots, raisins, and mayonnaise in bowl. Chill.

Serves 6—

GLAZED CARROTS

WHAT YOU NEED:

1 bag of peeled baby carrots (1 lb.)

1 Tbsp. margarine

1 Tbsp. orange marmalade

Salt and pepper to taste

Pot
Mixing spoon
Frying pan
Measuring spoon
Pot holder

WHAT YOU DO:

1. Place carrots in pot with water to cover. Bring to a boil and cook until slightly soft. Drain water.

2. Melt margarine in frying pan. Add carrots, marmalade, salt, and pepper. Heat and stir until glazed.

Serves 4—

E-Z TSIMMES

WHAT YOU NEED:

1 large can of sliced carrots

1 large can of sweet potatoes

3 apples

½ cup brown sugar

3 Tbsp. margarine, softened

1 cup water

Salt and pepper

Vegetable peeler
Knife and cutting board
Can opener
Colander
Measuring cup and spoon
Baking pan
Pot and mixing spoon
Foil wrap
Pot holder
Timer

WHAT YOU DO:

1. Preheat oven to 350°.

2. Drain carrots and sweet potatoes in colander.

3. Peel, core, and slice apples.

4. Arrange vegetables and apples in shallow baking pan.

5. In a pot, mix together sugar, margarine, water, salt, and pepper. Warm until sugar and margarine are melted. Pour over vegetables and apples.

6. Cover pan with foil and bake at 350° for 30 minutes.

Serves 4–6

E-Z POTATO PUDDING

WHAT YOU NEED:

2 eggs
2 cups water
¼ cup oil
6 oz. box potato pancake mix
¼ cup matzah meal
Oil or nonstick spray for pan

Mixing bowl and spoon
Eggbeater or whisk
Baking pan
Measuring cups
Pot holder
Timer

WHAT YOU DO:

1. Preheat oven to 450°.

2. Beat eggs until well-blended. Add water and oil, and mix well.

3. Stir in potato pancake mix and matzah meal. Allow to thicken for five minutes.

4. Spread mixture into well-oiled baking pan. Bake for 1 hour or until brown.

Serves 6–

BLENDER POTATO PANCAKES

WHAT YOU NEED:

2 eggs
1 small onion, peeled and quartered
1½ tsp. salt
3–4 medium potatoes, peeled or
    washed well, cut into quarters
¼ cup matzah meal
¼ cup oil for frying

Knife and cutting board
Measuring cup and spoon
Blender or food processor
Spoon
Frying pan and spatula
Paper towels
Pot holder

WHAT YOU DO:

1. Put all ingredients except oil into blender or food processor. Process until lumps disappear.

2. Heat oil in frying pan.

3. Drop by spoonfuls into pan, and fry over medium heat until brown on both sides.

4. Drain on paper towels.

5. Serve with applesauce.

Serves 3–

PEACH KUGEL

WHAT YOU NEED:

1-1 lb. box matzah farfel

2 sticks margarine, melted

2-1 lb. cans sliced peaches in syrup

7 eggs

1 c. sugar

1 tsp. vanilla

/4 tsp. salt

Cinnamon to taste

Nonstick spray or oil for pan

Large mixing bowl and spoon

Small bowls

Measuring cups and spoons

Can opener

Colander

Eggbeater or whisk

Baking pan

Pot holder

Timer

WHAT YOU DO:

1. Preheat oven to 350°.

2. Place farfel in colander and pour hot water over it. Drain and set aside.

3. Melt margarine in bowl in microwave or in pot on stove.

4. Drain peaches, reserving liquid.

5. Beat eggs in large bowl. Add melted margarine, sugar, vanilla, salt, farfel, and liquid from peaches. Mix well.

6. Spray baking pan and pour in half the batter. Add half the peaches and press them down into the batter. Pour remaining batter over the peaches and add the rest of the peaches on top. Sprinkle with cinnamon.

7. Bake for 1 hour or until brown.

Serves 8–10

E-Z CHEESY EGGPLANT PARMESAN

WHAT YOU NEED:

1 eggplant

2-16 oz. cans or jars tomato-mushroom sauce

Garlic and onion powder to taste

½ cup matzah meal

½ lb. sliced cheese

Knife and cutting board
Vegetable peeler
Can opener
Baking pan
Pot holder
Timer

WHAT YOU DO:

1. Preheat oven to 350°.

2. Peel eggplant and slice ½ inch thick.

3. In baking pan, alternate layers of sauce sprinkled with garlic and/or onion powder, eggplant, matzah meal, and cheese (in this order).

4. Bake for 20–25 minutes.

Serves 4–6

MEAT AND POULTRY

HOT DOG KABOBS

WHAT YOU NEED:

1 hot dog

4 cherry tomatoes

½ green pepper, cut into 4 chunks

Toothpicks
Baking sheet
Knife and cutting board
Pot holder
Timer

WHAT YOU DO:

1. Cut hot dog into 4 pieces. Put one piece on each toothpick. Add cherry tomato and green pepper chunk to each.

2. Broil in oven or toaster oven for 5 minutes or until hot dog browns.

Serves 1

SALAMI LATKES

WHAT YOU NEED:

2 eggs

½ cup water

½ cup matzah meal

½ cup diced salami or bologna

Oil for frying

Knife and cutting board
Eggbeater or whisk
Measuring cup
Mixing bowl and spoon
Frying pan and spatula
Pot holder
Paper towels

WHAT YOU DO:

1. Beat eggs. Add water and matzah meal and mix well. Add salami and mix again.

2. Heat oil in frying pan. Drop batter by spoonfuls into pan. Fry until brown on both sides.

3. Drain on paper towels. Serve with applesauce.

Serves 2

MEATBALLS

WHAT YOU NEED:

1 lb. ground beef

1 small onion, diced

1 egg

2 Tbsp. water

16 oz. can or jar tomato sauce

Mixing bowl and spoon
Knife and cutting board
Measuring spoons
Saucepan with lid
Can opener
Pot holder

WHAT YOU DO:

1. Put meat, onion, egg, and water in a bowl and mix well.

2. Put tomato sauce in saucepan and heat. Wet hands and form meatballs. Drop into sauce. Cover and simmer for 45 minutes.

Serves 3–4

MEAT LOAF

WHAT YOU NEED:

1 lb. lean ground beef

1 egg, beaten

1/2 package Passover onion soup mix

16 oz. can or jar tomato-mushroom
    sauce

1/4 cup matzah meal

Mixing bowl and spoon
Measuring cup
Loaf pan
Can opener
Pot holder
Timer

WHAT YOU DO:

1. Preheat oven to 350°.

2. In large bowl, put meat, egg, soup mix, 1/2 can of sauce, and matzah meal. Mix until well blended.

3. Place mixture in loaf pan, and pour remaining sauce over the top.

4. Bake for 1 hour or until brown. Drain any fat.

Serves 4

APRICOT CHICKEN 🍲🍲

WHAT YOU NEED:

5–6 lbs. chicken pieces

8 oz. bottle Russian salad dressing

I package Passover onion soup mix

10 oz. jar apricot preserves

Mixing bowl and spoon
Baking pan
Pot holder
Timer

WHAT YOU DO:

1. Preheat oven to 350°.

2. Rinse chicken pieces and pat dry. Place in baking pan.

3. Mix salad dressing, soup mix, and preserves in bowl. Pour over chicken. Marinate for a few hours or overnight.

4. Bake uncovered for 1 hour or until browned. Baste occasionally.

Serves 4–6

OVEN-BAKED CHICKEN 🍲🍲

WHAT YOU NEED:

I cup melted margarine mixed with I chopped garlic clove

2 cups matzah meal mixed with salt and pepper to taste

I cut-up fryer or package of boneless chicken breasts

Knife and cutting board
Bowls
Measuring cups
Baking pan
Pot holder
Timer

WHAT YOU DO:

1. Preheat oven to 350°

2. Melt margarine in microwave or in a pot on the stove. Add chopped garlic.

3. Put matzah meal in a separate bowl. Add salt and pepper.

4. Rinse and pat chicken dry. Dip into margarine mixture and then into seasoned matzah meal.

5. Place in baking dish and pour remaining margarine mixture over top. Bake 30–45 minutes until crispy.

Serves 3–4

CHICKEN SHAKE

WHAT YOU NEED:*

1 chicken, cut into serving pieces

½ cup Italian salad dressing

1 cup matzah meal

Salt, pepper, paprika, garlic powder

Mixing bowl and spoon

Measuring cup

Plastic bag

Roasting pan

Pot holder

Timer

WHAT YOU DO:

1. Preheat oven to 375°.

2. Put chicken pieces in shallow bowl. Pour salad dressing over chicken and stir until all the pieces are covered.

3. Put matzah meal and spices into plastic bag. Add chicken pieces, two at a time. Hold bag closed and shake to coat chicken. Arrange coated pieces in one layer in roasting pan.

4. Bake for 45 minutes to 1 hour.

*Shortcut: Buy prepared Passover chicken coating and follow package directions.

Serves 4

43

VEAL OR CHICKEN CUTLETS IN TOMATO SAUCE

WHAT YOU NEED:

6 veal or chicken cutlets, pounded thin

Salt and pepper to taste

2 eggs, beaten

I cup matzah meal

I cup cake meal

Oil for frying

16 oz. can or jar tomato sauce

Mallet or rolling pin

Plastic bag or waxed paper

Fork or whisk

3 bowls

Measuring cup

Frying pan and spatula

Paper towels

Baking pan

Pot holder

Timer

WHAT YOU DO:

1. Place cutlets in plastic bag or between sheets of waxed paper and pound thin with mallet or rolling pin. Season with salt and pepper.

2. Beat eggs in one bowl. Put matzah meal and cake meal in each of the other two bowls.

3. Heat oil in frying pan. Dip cutlets into cake meal, then beaten eggs, then matzah meal. Brown on both sides. Drain on paper towels.

4. Preheat oven to 350°. Put cutlets in baking pan, pour tomato sauce over them, and bake ½ hour or until bubbly.

Serves 3–6.

Meals
from Around
the
World

MATZAH PIZZA

WHAT YOU NEED:

1 round tea matzah (or regular matzah)

3–4 Tbsp. tomato sauce

2–3 slices cheese

Oregano, and/or garlic powder, to taste
   (optional)

Oil or nonstick spray for baking sheet

Baking sheet
Spoon and knife
Spatula
Pot holder
Timer

WHAT YOU DO:

1. Preheat oven to 350°.

2. Spread tomato sauce on matzah. Top with sliced cheese. Sprinkle with spices.

3. Put matzah on oiled baking sheet. Bake for about 5 minutes or until cheese melts.

Serves 1

TOSTADO

WHAT YOU NEED:

1 round tea matzah (or regular matzah)

1 Tbsp. oil

2 slices cheese, cut up

¼ cup shredded lettuce

¼ cup cubed tomato

1 Tbsp. chopped scallions

1 Tbsp. chopped green pepper

1 Tbsp. sour cream

Pastry brush

Baking sheet

Knife and cutting board

Spatula

Spoon

Pot holder

Timer

WHAT YOU DO:

1. Preheat oven to 300°.

2. Brush matzah with oil and warm in oven for 5 minutes.

3. Cover with cheese and vegetables. Top with sour cream.

Serves 1

HORSERADISH SALSA

WHAT YOU NEED:

1 red pepper

1 cooked carrot, diced

1 tomato, diced

1 small onion, diced

1 stalk celery, diced

½–1 cup prepared horseradish
(depending on how spicy you want it)

2–3 Tbsp. parsley, cilantro, and/or basil, chopped

Knife and cutting board

Measuring spoon

Mixing bowl and spoon

Foil

Pot holder

WHAT YOU DO:

1. Wrap red pepper in foil and roast in 350° oven until soft. Peel, seed, and dice.

2. Dice rest of vegetables and mix together with horseradish and spices.

3. Chill. Eat with gefilte fish or use as a dip with crackers or potato chips.

MATZAH EGG FOO YOUNG

WHAT YOU NEED:

1 package frozen chopped spinach

¼ cup mushrooms, sliced

1 onion, chopped

½ cup chopped celery

2 carrots, peeled and grated

2 Tbsp. butter or margarine

3 eggs

¼ cup matzah meal

1 tsp. salt

Dash of pepper

Oil for frying

WHAT YOU DO:

1. Cook and drain spinach according to package directions.

2. In a frying pan, saute mushrooms, onion, celery, and carrots in margarine until soft (5–8 minutes). Cool.

3. Put all ingredients in a bowl and mix well. Refrigerate 15 minutes.

4. Form into pancakes and fry in hot oil until brown on both sides.

Serves 3—

Covered saucepan

Colander

Vegetable peeler

Grater

Eggbeater or whisk

Knife and cutting board

Frying pan and spatula

Measuring cup and spoons

Mixing bowl and spoon

EGG DROP SOUP

WHAT YOU NEED:

3 cups chicken broth

1 egg, beaten lightly with fork

Handful of watercress, spinach, or lettuce

2 tsp. potato starch mixed with 2 Tbsp. water

WHAT YOU DO:

1. In a pot, bring the broth to a boil.

2. Mix the potato starch and water, and add to the soup. Stir until it thickens slightly.

3. Beat the egg and add it to the soup slowly while stirring. Add the greens and serve.

Pot

Measuring cup and spoons

Bowl

Fork

HAWAIIAN MATZAH FRY [D/P] [D/P] [D/P]

WHAT YOU NEED:

5 matzah

1 cup crushed pineapple

3 eggs

¼ cup shredded coconut

2–3 Tbsp. margarine

¼ tsp. cinnamon

2 Tbsp. sugar

Can opener
Bowls
Spoon
Measuring cup and spoons
Eggbeater or whisk
Frying pan and spatula

WHAT YOU DO:

1. Crumble matzah into bowl and add pineapple with juice.

2. Beat eggs and add to matzah. Stir in coconut.

3. Heat butter or margarine in frying pan. Pour in matzah mixture and cook until brown on one side. Flip and brown on other side. Sprinkle with cinnamon and sugar.

Serves 4—6

FINGER-DIPPING FONDUE

WHAT YOU NEED:

2 matzah

4 oz. processed cheese

½ cup milk

Salt, pepper, paprika

Saucepan or double boiler
Wooden spoon
Plates and bowls

WHAT YOU DO:

1. Break matzah into bite-size pieces and arrange on four small plates.

2. Melt cheese over low heat (or on top of double boiler). Add milk and seasonings. Stir with wooden spoon until smooth.

3. Pour cheese mixture into 4 small bowls and put each bowl on a plate of matzah. This is finger-dipping fun!

Serves ◄

DESSERTS AND SNACKS

CHOCOLATE CHIP COOKIES

WHAT YOU NEED:

1½ cup brown sugar, firmly packed
½ cup sugar
1 cup (2 sticks) margarine, softened
1 tsp. vanilla
2 eggs
¼ tsp. salt
½ cup matzah meal
½ cup cake meal
1 cup potato starch
1½ cup chocolate chips

Mixing bowl and spoon
Eggbeater or whisk
Measuring cups and spoon
Baking sheets
Baking parchment
Pot holder
Timer

WHAT YOU DO:

1. Put sugars and margarine in a bowl. Cream until smooth. Beat in eggs and vanilla.

2. Stir in salt, matzah and cake meals, potato starch, and chocolate chips.

3. Chill the dough OVERNIGHT.

4. Preheat oven to 350°.

5. Line baking sheets with parchment. Place scant teaspoons of batter on the sheets. Cookies should be small and spaced far apart to leave room for them to spread.

6. Bake for 10–12 minutes. Allow to cool before removing from parchment.

Makes 7–8 dozen cookies

PASSOVER ICE-BOX COOKIES

WHAT YOU NEED:

cup sugar

½ cup (1 stick) margarine

egg

Tbsp. orange juice

¼ tsp. salt

cup cake meal

½ cup chopped nuts

Mixing bowl and spoon

Measuring cup and spoon

Eggbeater or whisk

Knife and cutting board

Waxed paper

Cookie sheet

Spatula

Pot holder

Timer

WHAT YOU DO:

1. Put sugar and margarine in a bowl. Cream until smooth.

2. Add egg and juice, and beat well. Fold in dry ingredients and nuts.

3. Shape dough into sausages, wrap in waxed paper, and refrigerate for 2 or more hours. (The dough will keep for several days.)

4. Preheat oven to 350°. Slice dough into rounds and bake on ungreased cookie sheet for 15 minutes or until golden.

Makes 3 dozen

QUICK MACAROONS

WHAT YOU NEED:

5 cups flaked coconut

can (14 oz.) sweetened condensed milk

tsp. vanilla

½ cup chopped nuts

Margarine or nonstick spray for cookie sheet

Bowl

Measuring cup and spoon

Can opener

Cookie sheet

Spatula

Pot holder

Timer

WHAT YOU DO:

1. Preheat oven to 350°.

2. Mix ingredients together in bowl. Make sure they are mixed well.

3. Drop by teaspoonfuls onto lightly greased cookie sheet.

4. Bake for about 15 minutes or until lightly browned.

Makes 3 dozen

MERINGUE KISSES [D/P] [D/P]

WHAT YOU NEED:

½ cup sugar

3 egg whites

Chocolate kisses

Margarine (to grease cookie sheet)

Eggbeater or whisk

Mixing bowl and spoon

Measuring cup

Cookie sheet

Spatula

Pot holder

Timer

WHAT YOU DO:

1. Preheat oven to 350°.

2. Separate eggs (ask a grownup to help you) and save yolks for another use.

3. Beat egg whites until foamy.

4. Gradually beat in sugar and continue beating until egg whites are stiff and stand in peaks.

5. Drop by teaspoonfuls onto greased cookie sheet.

6. Put a chocolate kiss on top of each.

7. Bake 30 minutes or until meringue is hard.

Makes 12–18

STRAWBERRY MOUSSE 🅿️

WHAT YOU NEED:

2 egg whites

½ cup sugar

1 package frozen strawberries

Pinch of salt

Bowl and spoon
Eggbeater
Measuring cup
Freezer container

WHAT YOU DO:

1. Separate eggs (ask a grownup to help) and save yolks for another use.

2. Beat egg whites until stiff. Beat in sugar.

3. Add berries and salt and beat for at least 10 minutes.

4. Pour into serving dish and freeze. Thaw slightly before serving.

Serves 2–3

FROZEN FRUIT YOGURT POPSICLES 🄳

WHAT YOU NEED:

2 cups plain yogurt

1 small can frozen concentrated fruit juice (orange or pineapple)

2 tsp. vanilla

Bowl and spoon
Measuring cup and spoon
Popsicle holders or paper cups
Popsicle sticks

WHAT YOU DO:

1. Thaw frozen juice.

2. Combine all ingredients in a bowl and mix well.

3. Pour into popsicle holders or paper cups. (If you use cups, wait until pops are almost frozen, then put in sticks). You can also make "cube" pops in ice cube trays.

55

APPLE CAKE

WHAT YOU NEED:

3 eggs

½ cup oil

¼ cup orange juice

1 cup sugar

1 cup cake meal

½ tsp. salt

Nonstick spray or oil for pan

4 apples, peeled and sliced

cherry jam (optional)

cinnamon and sugar

Mixing bowls and spoon
Eggbeater or whisk
Measuring cup and spoons
Knife and cutting board
Vegetable peeler
8" or 9" square baking pan
Pot holder
Timer

WHAT YOU DO:

1. Preheat oven to 375°.

2. Beat eggs well.

3. Add oil, orange juice, and sugar and continue beating.

4. Stir in cake meal and salt.

5. Spread half the batter in a baking pan, cover with the apples. Dot with cherry jam (optional). Add the rest of the batter. Sprinkle with cinnamon and sugar.

6. Bake for 35–40 minutes.

For a lighter cake, separate the eggs. Beat whites separately and fold into the batter after mixing in cake meal and salt.

QUICK STRAWBERRY LAYER CAKE

WHAT YOU NEED:

1 Passover sponge cake

1 jar strawberry jam or preserves

1 package fresh or frozen strawberries

Serving dish
Knife
Spoon
Spatula

WHAT YOU DO:

1. Cut sponge cake in half lengthwise.

2. Place one layer on a serving dish. Spread strawberry jam and top with strawberries.

3. Place second layer on top and repeat.

Serves 6–8

TOFFEE SQUARES

WHAT YOU NEED:

1 cup (2 sticks) butter or margarine

1 egg

1 tsp. vanilla

1 cup sugar

1 cup cake meal

1 tsp. salt

Nonstick spray or oil for pan

1 package semi-sweet chocolate chips

½ cup chopped nuts (optional)

Mixing bowls and spoon

Measuring cup and spoons

10" x 13" jelly roll pan

Spatula

Pot holder

Timer

Knife

WHAT YOU DO:

1. Preheat oven to 350°.

2. Mix first six ingredients together. Stir until well blended.

3. Press dough into bottom of oiled pan.

4. Bake for 20–25 minutes or until golden brown.

5. Remove from oven. Quickly sprinkle chocolate chips on the hot dough, and return to the oven for about a minute.

6. Remove from oven and spread chocolate with a spatula. Sprinkle nuts on top.

7. Cool. Cut into squares.

CHOCOLATE NUT BARK ▣▣

WHAT YOU NEED:

12 oz. package chocolate chips (or
  chopped chocolate bar)
1 cup whole almonds

Saucepan or double boiler
Cookie sheet
Waxed paper
Mixing spoon
Measuring cup

WHAT YOU DO:

1. Melt chocolate over low heat. Stir to prevent burning.

2. Toast almonds until light brown (you can use toaster oven), and add to chocolate.

3. Spread mixture over cookie sheet lined with waxed paper.

4. Chill until firm and break into pieces.

T.V. MUNCH ▣

WHAT YOU NEED:

1 cup dried apples
1 cup dried pears
1 cup dried pineapple
1 cup raisins
1 cup almonds or walnuts
1 cup chocolate bits

Bowl
Measuring cup

WHAT YOU DO:

1. Put all ingredients in a bowl and mix.

2. Turn on T.V. and munch!

CHOCOLATE MATZAH

WHAT YOU NEED:

12 oz. package chocolate chips (or
    chopped chocolate bar)

1 Tbsp. margarine

4 matzah

Saucepan or double boiler
Mixing spoon
Measuring spoon
Rolling pin
Cookie sheet
Waxed paper
Pot holder

WHAT YOU DO:

1. Melt chocolate and margarine over low heat. Stir to prevent burning.

2. Break matzah into pieces and stir into chocolate.

3. Cover a cookie sheet with waxed paper.

4. Pour chocolate matzah mixture onto waxed paper and cover with another sheet of waxed paper.

5. Flatten mixture with rolling pin. Refrigerate.

6. When mixture hardens, peel off top paper and break chocolate into pieces.

CHOCOLATE NUT-RAISIN CLUSTERS

WHAT YOU NEED:

6 oz. package chocolate chips (or
    chopped chocolate bar)

1½ cups shelled walnuts

1 cup raisins

Spoon
Saucepan or double boiler
Measuring cup
Waxed paper
Pot holder

WHAT YOU DO:

1. Melt chocolate over warm water in double boiler, or in saucepan over low heat.

2. Stir in nuts and raisins.

3. Drop by teaspoonfuls onto waxed paper and chill.

Makes 12–18

CHOCOLATE-COVERED FRUIT

WHAT YOU NEED:

Use strawberries, slices of orange, and
chunks of apple, pear, bananas, and/or
pineapple

12 oz. package of chocolate chips

3 Tbsp. margarine

Saucepan or double boiler
Toothpicks
Waxed paper
Pot holder

WHAT YOU DO:

1. Melt chocolate and margarine on
top of stove in saucepan or double
boiler. Use low heat and stir to
prevent burning.

2. Put fruit on toothpicks and dip into
chocolate. Place on waxed paper and
chill in refrigerator until chocolate
hardens.

Shakes
AND
Coolers

FRUIT SHAKE

WHAT YOU NEED:

2 cups milk

Choose from: I banana, sliced; I cup
    fresh or frozen berries; or I cup
    sliced peaches or melon

I Tbsp. honey

Knife and cutting board
Measuring cup and spoon
Blender
Glass

WHAT YOU DO:

1. Place all ingredients into blender
   and whip on medium speed until
   well mixed.

2. Pour into tall glass and enjoy.

CHOCOLATE EGG CREAM

WHAT YOU NEED:

2 Tbsp. chocolate syrup

½ cup milk

1½ c. club soda

Spoon
Glass

WHAT YOU DO:

1. Pour milk into glass and stir in
   chocolate syrup. Add club soda to top
   of glass.

COOLERS

GRAPE SPRITZER
Fill a glass half full with grape juice.
Add club soda and stir.

LEMONADE
In a small pitcher, combine 2 cups
club soda, ½ cup lemon juice and 2
tablespoons honey. Add ice and mix.

Measuring cup and spoon
Spoon
Glass
Pitcher

In loving memory of Grandma Estelle who taught me the importance of family traditions. My deepest thanks to my mom, Anne, for her love, encouragement, support, and the wonderful memories of Passover dinners we have shared; and to my husband, Marv, my children and grandchildren, for giving me the inspiration to write this book.

—B.S.

To my mom, Miriam, for instilling in me her love of Judaism; and to my grandchildren, Max, Isabel, Alex, and Sam, who will continue our Jewish tradition.

—J.T.

Illustrations by Bill Hauser

Text copyright © 1985, 2004 by Judy Tabs and Barbara Steinberg
Illustrations copyright © 2004 by Kar-Ben Publishing, Inc.

KAR-BEN PUBLISHING, INC.
A division of Lerner Publishing Group
241 First Avenue North
Minneapolis, MN 55401 U.S.A.
800-4KARBEN

Website address: www.karben.com

Library of Congress Cataloging-in-Publication Data

Tabs, Judy.
     Matzah meals : a Passover cookbook for kids / by Judy Tabs and Barbara Steinberg ; pictures by Bill Hauser.
         p.   cm.
     Summary: A Passover cookbook with an emphasis on matzos that includes crafts for and information on Passover and the Seder.
     ISBN: 1–58013–086–0 (pbk. : alk. paper)
     1. Passover cookery—Juvenile literature. 2. Matzos—Juvenile literature. 3. Seder—Juvenile literature. [1. Passover cookery. 2. Matzos. 3. Seder. 4. Passover. 5. Holidays.]
     I. Steinberg, Barbara. II. Hauser, Bill, ill. III. Title.
     TX724.T33 2004
     641.5'676—dc22   2003015259

Manufactured in the United States of America
2 3 4 5 6 7 – JR – 10 09 08 07 06 05